Amphibians

Heather Hammonds

Chapter 1	Amphibians	2
Chapter 2	Frogs and Toads	6
Chapter 3	Salamanders and Newts	12
Chapter 4	Caecilians	18
Chapter 5	Amphibians in Danger	20
Chapter 6	Amphibians as Pets	22
Glossary and Index		24

MW00652164

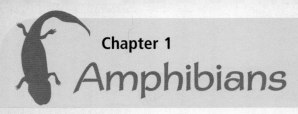

Chapter 1
Amphibians

Are there frogs in a pond near you? Have you heard them croaking?

Frogs are amphibians. Amphibians are **cold-blooded** animals. They have a bony skeleton and soft, **moist** skin.

There are lots of different kinds of amphibians. The main groups of amphibians are:

• frogs and toads

• salamanders and newts

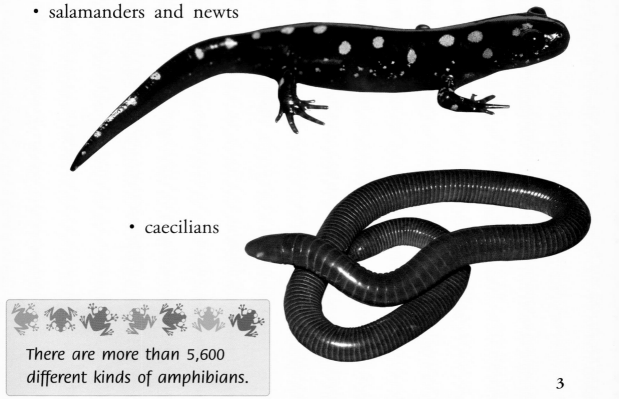

• caecilians

There are more than 5,600 different kinds of amphibians.

3

Most amphibians live in water and on land.

However there are also amphibians that live only in water, amphibians that live under the ground, and amphibians that live in trees.

A clown tree frog lives in trees.

Amazing Changes

Most amphibians lay eggs in water. After the eggs hatch, the babies live in the water.

They breathe through **gills**. As the babies grow older, their legs grow. They also grow lungs and their gills disappear. Now they are able to leave the water.

A Frog Life Cycle

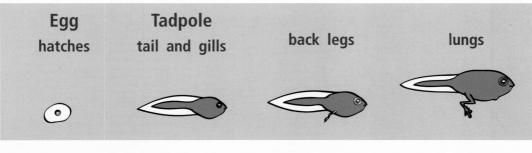

Egg
hatches

Tadpole
tail and gills

back legs

lungs

front legs

Froglet
young frog

Adult Frog

A few kinds of amphibians do not lose their gills.
They stay in the water and just grow bigger.

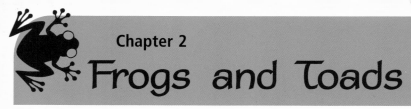

Chapter 2
Frogs and Toads

Frogs and toads are amphibians with four legs and no tails.

Frogs have smooth skin and long, strong back legs that help them to hop.

Frogs usually lay their eggs in clusters. When the eggs hatch, the baby frogs are called tadpoles.

a cluster of frog eggs

a striped marsh frog

an Asian toad

Toads have thick, bumpy skin that is drier than frogs' skin.

Toads have short bodies and short back legs. Because their back legs are shorter, they cannot hop as far as frogs.

Toads lay their eggs in long chains. When the eggs hatch, the baby toads are also called tadpoles.

chains of toad eggs

Clusters of frog eggs are called frog spawn.
Chains of toad eggs are called toad spawn.

7

Green Tree Frog

Green tree frogs have bright green skin and golden eyes.

During the day, they hide in cool places close to water. At night they come out and catch insects to eat.

Green tree frogs have special round pads on their fingers and toes to help them climb things.

Wood Frog

Most animals would die if their bodies froze and turned to ice. Wood frogs don't die if this happens to them!

Wood frogs **hibernate** during winter. In colder places, much of a wood frog's body becomes frozen. When the ice melts in the spring, the frog wakes up and hops away!

Like all frogs, only male wood frogs croak. They croak to call female frogs to **mate** with them.

Cane Toad

Cane toads are very large amphibians that can grow to more than 7 inches long.

In some parts of the world, cane toads are pests. They eat lots of insects and small animals. **Native** frogs and toads cannot live in the same place as cane toads.

Cane toads are also very **poisonous** and can poison animals that try to eat them.

Eastern Spadefoot Toad

Eastern spadefoot toads live underground in burrows. They have sharp, little, spade-like parts that stick out on their back feet. They use these **spades** to dig their burrows.

Eastern spadefoot toads live underground in dry weather, but when it rains they all come out together. The female toads lay eggs in pools of rainwater.

Eastern spadefoot toads can stay underground for several weeks at a time.

Chapter 3
Salamanders and Newts

Salamanders and newts are amphibians with four legs and long tails. All newts are salamanders. Newt is the name used for some kinds of salamanders.

Most newts spend more time living in water than salamanders do.

a tiger salamander

Salamanders and newts look a little bit like lizards. However they do not have scales.

They have soft, moist skin like other amphibians.

Salamanders and newts generally lay their eggs in water.

a northern red salamander

salamander eggs

Many salamanders lay their eggs one at a time. They do not lay them in clusters or chains, like frogs and toads.

13

Pacific Giant Salamander

Pacific giant salamanders live around cool lakes, rivers, and streams. They are very fierce and make a barking sound when disturbed.

Female Pacific giant salamanders lay their eggs in underwater nests. They guard the eggs for several months until they hatch.

Axolotl

Axolotls live in water and do not come out on land. Baby axolotls grow four legs after they hatch, but their gills do not disappear. Instead they continue to grow bigger until they reach adult size.

A newly hatched axolotl is called a larva. The babies of other salamanders and newts are also called larvae.

15

Great Crested Newt

Great crested newts are large, dark-colored newts with orange or yellow bellies.

Male great crested newts grow a large **crest** on their back in the **breeding season**. At this time, they also do a special dance in front of female newts before they mate with them.

Rough-skinned Newt

Rough-skinned newts live in cool, damp forests. They have dry warty skin for most of the year, but in the breeding season, male rough-skinned newts change. For a short time, their skin becomes smooth.

Rough-skinned newts have very poisonous skin.

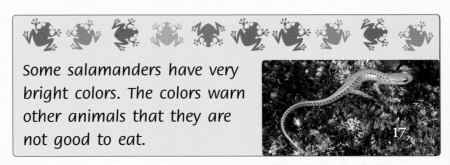

Some salamanders have very bright colors. The colors warn other animals that they are not good to eat.

Caecilians

...lians are long, thin amphibians with no legs. Sometimes caecilians are mistaken for worms or snakes.

All caecilians have small **tentacles** on their heads. The tentacles probably help them to smell things.

Caecilians generally live underground. However some live in water.

Rubber Eels

Rubber eels are caecilians that only live in water. They eat worms and other small water animals.

Rubber eels cannot see well and hunt for their food by smell.

Rubber eels are often kept as pets in aquariums.

Rubber eels are sometimes called rubber worms or caecilian worms.

Chapter 5

Amphibians in Danger

Lots of amphibians around the world are **endangered**. Sadly they are disappearing from places where they once lived.

Pollution in rivers, lakes, and ponds harms amphibians.

When lakes and ponds are filled in to build roads or houses, amphibians lose their homes.

People are working together to help save amphibians. They:

- study amphibians
- help look after the places where they live
- help look after sick amphibians
- teach others about them

In some places, a skin disease is making frogs very sick. Scientists are working hard to find a way to stop the disease.

Chapter 6

Amphibians as Pets

Some amphibians can be kept as pets.

It takes a lot of work to care for amphibians. They need:

- a large, clean tank to live in
- lots of insects to eat
- clean water, if they live only in water
- both water and land, if they live on land, too.

Sometimes tadpoles are kept in a tank at school. Everyone in the class can study the tadpoles. Students can learn about the frog life cycle. They can watch the tadpoles slowly turn into frogs!

Amphibians are also kept at zoos.

Glossary

breeding season   the time of the year when amphibians or other animals mate

cold-blooded   when an animal cannot make its own body heat and its temperature changes with its surroundings

crest   a growth on the back or head of an animal

endangered   at risk of dying out

gills   special body parts that let water animals breathe air from water

hibernate   to spend the winter in a very deep sleep

mate   when a male and female join together to make babies

moist   wet or damp

native   belonging to or coming from a place

poisonous   harmful; able to cause sickness or death

pollution   harmful materials that get into water and land, and poison them

spades   tools for digging; shovels

tentacles   long growths on the head of an animal

Index

cane toad 10

eastern spadefoot toad 11

great crested newt 16

green tree frog 8

Pacific giant salamander 14

rough-skinned newt 17

rubber eel 19

wood frog 9